Biodiversity

of Coasts

GREG PYERS

Marshall Cavendish
Benchmark
New York

Website: www.marshallcavendish.us

This publication represents the opinions and views of the author based on Greg Pyer's personal experience, knowledge, and research. The information in this book serves as a general guide only. The author and publisher have used their best efforts in preparing this book and disclaim liability rising directly and indirectly from the use and application of this book.

Other Marshall Cavendish Offices:
Marshall Cavendish Ltd. 5th Floor, 32-38 Saffron Hill, London EC1N 8 FH, UK • Marshall Cavendish International (Asia) Private Limited, 1 New Industrial Road, Singapore 536196 • Marshall Cavendish International (Thailand) Co Ltd. 253 Asoke, 12th Flr, Sukhumvit 21 Road, Klongtoey Nua, Wattana, Bangkok 10110, Thailand • Marshall Cavendish (Malaysia) Sdn Bhd, Times Subang, Lot 46, Subang Hi-Tech Industrial Park, Batu Tiga, 40000 Shah Alam, Selangor Darul Ehsan, Malaysia

Marshall Cavendish is a trademark of Times Publishing Limited

All websites were available and accurate when this book was sent to press.

Library of Congress Cataloging-in-Publication Data

Pyers, Greg.
    Biodiversity of coasts / Greg Pyers.
        p. cm. — (Biodiversity)
    Includes index.
    Summary: "Discusses the variety of living things in the ecosystem of a coast"—Provided by publisher.
    ISBN 978-1-60870-069-1
    1. Coastal organisms—Juvenile literature. 2. Coastal ecology—Juvenile literature.
    3. Endangered ecosystems—Juvenile literature. I. Title.
    QH95.7.P94 2010
    577.5'1—dc22

                                                                        2009042311

First published in 2010 by
MACMILLAN EDUCATION AUSTRALIA PTY LTD
15–19 Claremont Street, South Yarra 3141

Visit our website at www.macmillan.com.au or go directly to www.macmillanlibrary.com.au

Associated companies and representatives throughout the world.

Copyright © Greg Pyers 2010

Edited by Georgina Garner
Text and cover design by Kerri Wilson
Page layout by Kerri Wilson
Photo research by Legend Images
Illustrations by Richard Morden

Printed in China

Acknowledgments
The author and the publisher are grateful to the following for permission to reproduce copyright material:

Front cover photograph of the beach at Ecola State Park, Oregon, USA © Craig Tuttle/Corbis.
Back cover photograph of a Dalmatian pelican © Eric Isselée/Shutterstock.

Photographs courtesy of:
© Ashley Cooper/Corbis, 23; © Jamie Harron, Papilio/Corbis, 28; © Craig Tuttle/Corbis, 1; The DW Stock Picture Library, 19; Exxon Valdez Oil Spill Trustee Council, 20; Steve Winter/Getty Images, 25; © 2008 Jupiterimages Corporation, 9, 10 (centre), 11; Photolibrary/Stephen Alvarez, 24; Photolibrary/Phillip Hayson, 15; Photolibrary/IFA-BILDERTEAM GMBH, 27; Photolibrary/Suzanne Long, 21; Photolibrary/Nancy Sefton, 4; Image provided by the SeaWiFS Project, NASA/Goddard Space Flight Center, and ORBIMAGE, 8;© silvano audisio/Shutterstock, 17; © Ramon Berk/Shutterstock, 22; © Myszka Brudnicka/Shutterstock, 10 (bottom); © C. Daveney/Shutterstock, 16; © Yory Frenklakh/Shutterstock, 10 (top); © Jose Gil/Shutterstock, 13; © Igor Grochev/Shutterstock, 18; © mahout/Shutterstock, 29; © michael rubin/Shutterstock, 7.

Illustration on page 14 based on graphic at http://maps.grida.no/go/graphic/coastlines_under_threat [source: D. Bryant, E. Rodenburg, T. Cox and D. Nielsen, *Coastlines at Risk: an Index of Potential Development-Related Threats to Coastal Ecosystems*, World Resources Institute (WRI), Washington DC, 1996; designer: Philippe Rekacewicz, UNEP/GRID-Arendal].

While every care has been taken to trace and acknowledge copyright, the publisher tenders their apologies for any accidental infringement where copyright has proved untraceable. Where the attempt has been unsuccessful, the publisher welcomes information that would redress the situation.

Contents

Glossary Words

When a word is printed in **bold**, you can look up its meaning in the Glossary on page 31.

What Is Biodiversity?

Biodiversity, or biological diversity, describes the variety of living things in a particular place, in a particular **ecosystem**, or across the entire Earth.

Measuring Biodiversity

The biodiversity of a particular area is measured on three levels:

- **species** diversity, which is the number and variety of species in the area.
- genetic diversity, which is the variety of **genes** each species has. Genes determine the characteristics of different living things. A variety of genes within a species enables it to **adapt** to changes in its environment.
- ecosystem diversity, which is the variety of **habitats** in the area. A diverse ecosystem has many habitats within it.

Species Diversity

Species diversity changes from one habitat to another. Habitats, such as rain forests and coasts, have different levels of biodiversity. Within a coastal habitat, mussels and other shellfish cling to rocks close to the water's edge. Coastal grasses live above the high-tide mark, and seals rest on shore and hunt in the water. Some fish live entirely in rockpools.

Habitats and Ecosystems

There are many habitats along a coast. Some coastal habitats are cliffs, caves, rockpools, and sand dunes. Different kinds of **organisms** live in these habitats. The animals, plants, other living things, nonliving things, and all the ways they affect each other make up a coastal ecosystem.

Coastal habitats are biodiverse. They have many kinds of animals, including species of sea star and sea grass.

Biodiversity Under Threat

The variety of species on Earth is under threat. There are somewhere between 5 million and 30 million species on Earth. Most of these species are very small and hard to find, so only about 1.75 million have been described and named. These are called known species.

Scientists estimate that as many as fifty species become **extinct** every day. Extinction is a natural process, but human activities have sped up the rate of extinction by nearly one thousand times.

Known Species of Organisms on Earth

Algae 1%
Fungi 3%
Bacteria 1%
Plants 17%
Vertebrates 4%
Other invertebrates 6%
Invertebrates
Molluscs 5%
Arachnids 6%
Insects 57%

The known species of organisms on Earth can be divided into bacteria, algae, fungi, plant, and animal species. Animal species are further divided into vertebrates and invertebrates.

Approximate Numbers of Known Vertebrate Species

ANIMAL GROUP	KNOWN SPECIES
Fish	31,000
Birds	10,000
Reptiles	8,800
Amphibians	6,500
Mammals	5,500

Why Is Biodiversity Important?

Biodiversity is important for many reasons. The diverse organisms in an ecosystem take part in natural processes essential to the survival of all living things. Biodiversity produces food and medicine. It is also important to people's quality of life.

Natural Processes

Human survival depends on the natural processes that go on in ecosystems. Through natural processes, air and water are cleaned, waste is decomposed, **nutrients** are recycled, and disease is kept under control. Natural processes depend on the organisms that live in the soil, on the plants that produce oxygen and absorb **carbon dioxide**, and on the organisms that break down dead plants and animals. When species of organisms become extinct, natural processes may stop working.

Food

We depend on biodiversity for our food. The world's major food plants are grains, vegetables, and fruits. These plants have all been bred from plants in the wild. Wild plants are important sources of genes for breeding new disease-resistant crops. If these wild plants were to become extinct, their genes would be lost.

Medicine

About 40 percent of all prescription drugs come from chemicals that have been extracted from plants. Scientists discover new, useful plant chemicals every year. The National Cancer Institute discovered that 70 percent of plants found to have anticancer properties were rain forest plants.

When plant species become extinct, the chemicals within them are lost forever. The lost chemicals might have been important in making new medicines.

The Potato Plant

The potato plant is native to the Andes Mountains in South America. It was first brought to Europe in 1536 and, since then, potatoes have become the world's fourth most important food crop. To protect the potato's genetic diversity, the International Potato Center in Lima, Peru, keeps more than 4,500 varieties of potatoes in test tubes and cold storage.

Quality of Life

Biodiversity is important to our quality of life. Animals and plants inspire wonder. They are part of our **heritage**. Some species have become particularly important to us. If the tiger became extinct, our survival would not be affected, but we would feel great sadness and regret.

Animal species such as tigers inspire people's wonder and imagination. This improves their quality of life.

Extinct Species

North America's passenger pigeon was one of the most common birds in the world. Flocks could be so dense and so large that they blocked out the sun as they flew by. Due to hunting, the passenger pigeon population began to decline and then plummet. Attempts were made around 1900 to protect the pigeons, but they were too late. On September 1, 1914, the last known passenger pigeon died at Cincinnati Zoo, Ohio. When this species became extinct, Earth's biodiversity was reduced.

Coasts of the World

The coast is where the land meets the sea. A coast may have sandy beaches, rocky cliffs, stretches of swampy land, or coves and inlets. People live along coasts because they provide access to trade, transportation, and recreation.

The Length of Coastlines

The length of coastline throughout the world is estimated. There is somewhere between 310,500 and 521,600 miles (500,000 and 840,000 kilometers) of coastline. The difference in the estimates depends on how precisely all the twists and turns in a coastline are measured.

Countries With the Most Coastline

COUNTRY	APPROXIMATE LENGTH OF COASTLINE (miles)	PERCENTAGE OF WORLD TOTAL
Canada	150,000	29.0
Indonesia	34,000	6.5
Greenland	27,500	5.2
Russia	23,400	4.5
Philippines	22,500	4.3
Japan	18,500	3.5
Australia	16,000	3.1
Norway	13,600	2.6
United States	12,400	2.4
Total	**317,900**	**61.1**

Lengths of coastlines are difficult to measure because of their many twists and turns.

People and Coasts

More than 40 percent of the world's population, about 2.68 billion people, live within 37 miles (60 km) of a coast. Many of the world's largest cities and many towns are built along beachfronts.

The large number of people living along coasts places enormous pressure on coastal ecosystems and biodiversity. In some coastal areas, the human population more than doubles when tourists arrive for summer vacations. As the population increases, more housing, ports, and roads are needed. Pollution also increases.

The population of coastal areas around the world is expected to continue to increase in the future. This increase will have an impact on global coastal biodiversity.

Many tourists flock to coastal areas with sandy beaches during the summer.

Turtles and Urban Development

When **marine** turtles hatch, they emerge from their sandy nests and make their way to the sea. This can be dangerous on a coast that is populated by humans. Streetlights can confuse the young hatchlings. They mistake the lights for moonlight on the water and sometimes head inland instead of out to sea. Pet dogs that are allowed to wander along turtle beaches prey on turtle hatchlings, too.

Coastal Biodiversity

There are many types of coastal habitats, and different kinds of species are found in each of these habitats. Coastal habitats stretch several miles inland and out to sea.

Types of Coasts

There are three main types of coast. Each is a habitat for different species of animals and plants.

Rocky Coasts

Rocky coasts have cliffs and rocky **outcrops** that jut into the sea. Rocky coasts are hammered by waves and are constantly being worn away. Hardy plants cling to cracks in the rock and many seabirds nest on the cliffs and outcrops, safe from **predators**.

Rocky coast

Tidal Plain Coasts

Tidal plain coasts are swampy places with **mudflats** and mangrove forests. Much of the coast is covered at high tide. At low tide, crabs emerge from their burrows to feed. Shorebirds such as sandpipers probe the exposed mud with their beaks, looking for worms and other invertebrates.

Tidal plain coast

Beach Coasts

Beach and barrier coasts are sandy, with dunes covered by grasses and shrubs. Birds nest in the dunes, and marine turtles come ashore to lay their eggs in the sand.

Beach coast

Coastal Areas

The coast is not just the narrow area where the land meets the sea. It also includes the coastal zone and the continental shelf.

Coastal Zone

The coastal zone is the area where the land and the sea strongly affect each other. Salty winds that blow in from the sea may affect the types of plants that grow for several miles inland. Soil that washes into the sea from the land may affect marine animals and plants up to several miles out from the shoreline. Coral reefs can be killed when **silt** from the land smothers them. These inland and marine areas are part of the coastal zone.

Continental Shelf

The continental shelf is an area of seabed around a coast. The water is shallow along the continental shelf. The shelf may extend 250 miles (400 km) from the shoreline before it falls away to deeper ocean. Many species that live in these shallow waters are not found farther out to sea.

Sea Grass

Coastal waters are usually quite shallow. This means light penetrates to the seafloor, enabling sea grass to grow. These flowering plants are the main food of manatees. Sea grass grows best in sheltered water, which is found in coastal inlets where waves are calmed by reefs and shorelines.

Soil builds up in a coastal zone, where a river meets the sea.

Coastal Ecosystems

Living and nonliving things, and the **interactions** between them, make up coastal ecosystems. Living things are plants and animals. Nonliving things are rocks, sand, and water, as well as the **climate**, temperature, tides, and surf.

Food Chains and Food Webs

A very important way that different species interact is by eating or consuming other species. This transfers energy and nutrients from one organism to another. A food chain illustrates this flow of energy, by showing what eats what. A food web shows how different food chains fit together.

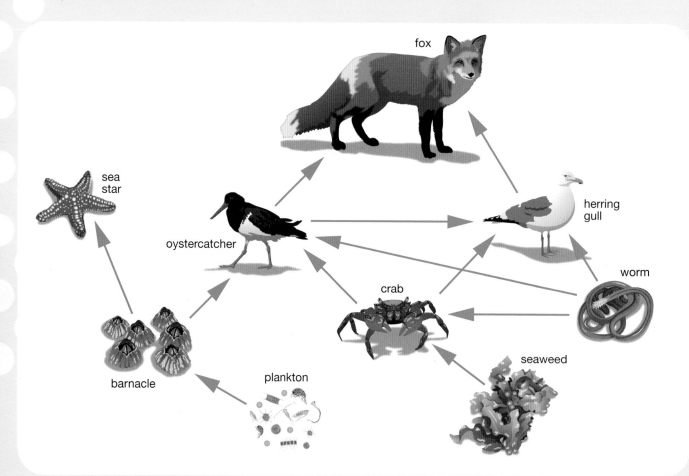

This coastal food web is made up of several food chains. In one food chain, seaweed is eaten by crabs, which in turn are eaten by oystercatchers.

Other Interactions

Living and nonliving things on a coast interact in other ways, too. While feeding on shellfish, sea otters keep themselves anchored in one place on the sea surface by wrapping **kelp** around their bodies. The kelp is attached to the seafloor. Seaweed crabs thread pieces of seaweed through hooked spines on their backs. This provides them with camouflage, which hides them from predators, such as oystercatchers, that hunt at low tide.

Tidal Interactions

There are two high tides and two low tides every twenty-four hours or so. Tides are very important to the daily lives of coastal animals. At high tide, stingrays swim into shallow water to feed on snails and other animals. As the tide goes out, the stingrays swim back to deeper water. Barnacles, animals that attach themselves to rocks and ship hulls, open their shells at high tide to catch **plankton** from the water. At low tide, they are exposed and they must close their shells tightly to keep from drying out in the air.

Mussels

Mussels are most numerous on rocks that are covered at high tide and exposed to the air at low tide. Mussels cannot live above the high tide line because they would be unable to feed on the plankton that live in the water. They are not numerous below the low tide line because sea stars will prey on them.

At low tide, when the sea has receded, thousands of mussels can be seen covering the rocks on this coast.

Threats to Coastal Biodiversity

Coastal biodiversity in many parts of the world is under severe threat due to human activities. Biodiversity is most at risk in coastal habitats such as mangroves and other coastal wetlands.

Human Threats

Urbanization, overfishing, land clearing, **invasive species**, changing climate, pollution, tourism, and shipping all contribute to the loss of coastal habitat and biodiversity. About 34 percent of the world's coasts are at severe risk of **degradation** due to the effects of human activity. Another 17 percent are at moderate risk. In Europe, 86 percent of the coasts are classified as being at either high or moderate risk of degradation. In Asia, 69 percent of the coasts are threatened.

Coastlines Under Threat

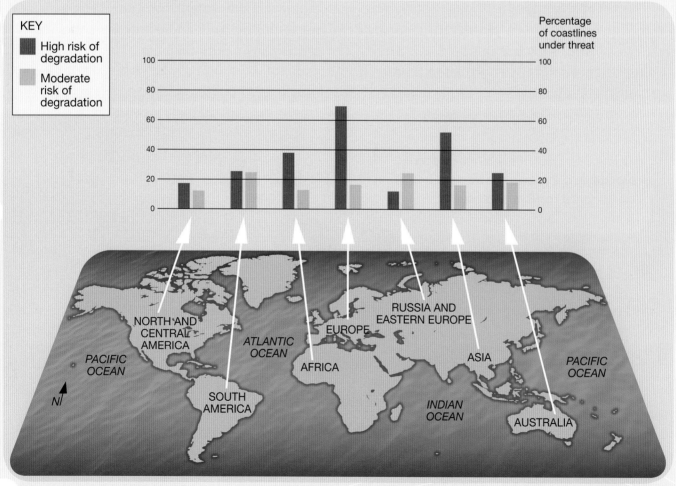

14

Mangroves

Mangroves are trees that grow in coastal mudflats. For many years, mangrove forests have been considered swampy wastelands. They are dense, muddy, and full of insects. Mangroves, however, are vitally important for many reasons. They absorb vast amounts of nutrients that wash down from the land. When mangrove forests are removed to build roads, marinas, hotels, and ports, these nutrients enter the sea and increase the growth of **algae**. Excessive algal growth can smother and kill corals. Mangroves also protect coastlines from huge waves caused by tropical storms. They are home to many animal species, including marine fish that feed among their roots at high tide.

Did You Know?

About 80 percent of the world's 13,000 or more species of marine fish are coastal. These species need coastal habitats, such as mangrove forests, in which to breed. Urban development of coastal areas has resulted in many mangrove forests being cleared.

Loss of Mangroves

Since 1800, more than half of the world's mangrove forests have been cleared. In 2007, fewer than 60,000 square miles (150,000 sq km) remained of an original 125,000 square miles (320,000 sq km). Half of this loss occurred in the last fifty years. Mangrove loss is due mainly to shrimp farming, urbanization, tourism, agriculture, and the construction of roads and ports.

Many cities on the Gold Coast in Queensland, Australia, were built on mudflats and mangroves.

BIODIVERSITY THREAT:
Urbanization

Urbanization poses many threats to coastal biodiversity. Towns and cities replace natural coastal habitats. Humans produce waste and engage in activities that can harm coastal animals and plants.

Building Towns and Cities

Coasts are the most urbanized places in the world. Traditionally, most trade has been by sea, so towns and cities have grown around ports. Many people like to live near the sea and many coasts have been urbanized as vacation houses are built. As the world's population increases, more and more of the coast is urbanized as roads, buildings, bridges, and other town and city features are built.

The features of towns and cities replace the natural features of the coast, such as the native **vegetation**, wetlands, and mudflats. Because of this, the biodiversity of the coast is changed. Many coastal animals and plants become endangered. Some become extinct.

Urban Waste

Where there are many people, a lot of waste is produced. This waste includes **sewage**, oil, and garbage. Sewage can cause the excessive growth of algae. Algae can kill coral reefs, which lie close to the coast. Oil washes down drains from streets and is poisonous to animals. Garbage, such as cigarette butts and plastic bags, can pollute the land and sea.

Storm water is piped directly into the sea, carrying with it waste from towns and cities.

Human Activities

Urbanization leads to more people using a coast. Human activity often has a negative effect on coastal habitats and coastal species.

Human activities can increase **erosion** in coastal areas. The coast is constantly changing. Waves bring cliffs down and wind blows sand dunes inland. These natural changes take place over many years, and animals and plants usually have time to adapt. When humans disturb these natural processes, such as by erecting breakwaters or building on dunes, erosion speeds up.

Humans may scare away or cause the death of coastal species, too. A beach that is busy with many swimmers and bathers is not a suitable habitat for birds or turtles that might nest there. Beachgoers often bring their dogs with them. An unattended dog can kill nesting shorebirds.

Human activities have reshaped the Mediterranean coast, such as the coast of Riomaggiore in Italy.

BIODIVERSITY THREAT:
Invasive Species

Invasive species are nonnative species that spread in large numbers and dominate native species. The biodiversity of many coastal ecosystems around the world is under threat from invasive species.

Stowaways

Many animal and plant species are carried from one part of the world to another, not deliberately, but as accidental stowaways in the **ballast** tanks of large ships. Many organisms in the ballast seawater are carried to foreign ports.

Before a ship takes on new cargo, its ballast tanks are emptied. The marine organisms that were carried in the ballast water enter the foreign sea. Many stowaway animals and plants die in the ballast tanks or soon after they are released in a foreign port. Others thrive in their new home and become serious pests. These organisms may thrive because their new environment is free of their natural predators or of other species that compete with them for food. The new species may overwhelm local species and disturb the ecosystem. Some of the local species disappear altogether.

Zebra Mussels

Zebra mussels reached North American coastal waters around 1986. They arrived from Europe in ballast water carried by ships. Zebra mussels have caused enormous damage to North American coastal ecosystems. They grow in densities of up to 200,000 mussels per square foot and crowd out native species.

A container ship often empties its ballast water in port as it takes on cargo.

Bitou bush is an invasive species in many coastal habitats.

Imported Invasive Species

Many invasive species have been released deliberately in coastal areas around the world. Between the 1940s and 1960s, a southern African coastal plant, the bitou bush, was planted in sand dunes along the southeastern coast of Australia. This was done to control dune erosion. Since then, bitou bush has spread along the coast, often overwhelming native plants. It is now a major pest that costs millions of dollars to control.

European Flat Oyster

The European flat oyster was deliberately introduced into the Atlantic Ocean near Maine so it could be harvested as food. It competes with local oysters. It can grow up to 8 inches (20 cm) long and live up to twenty years.

BIODIVERSITY THREAT:
Pollution

Pollution is a major threat to coastal biodiversity. Oil spills affect coastal ecosystems for many years. Cigarette butts and plastic litter washed from city streets choke and poison marine animals.

Oil Spills

Crude oil is transported around the world in huge tanker ships. Occasionally, there is an accident and one of these ships spills its cargo. Oil is toxic. When spilled, it gets into the fur and feathers of animals and sticks there. The fur or feathers no longer keep the animal warm and the animal soon dies of cold. Birds with oil-soaked feathers cannot fly.

When an oil-affected animal tries to clean itself, it swallows the oil and is poisoned. The oil enters food chains, causing stunted growth in salmon and reduced life expectancy in birds and mammals.

Oil-covered seabirds are recovered from the sea after a coastal oil spill.

Exxon Valdez Oil Spill

One of the worst oil spills occurred in March 1989 when the tanker *Exxon Valdez* ran aground on the coast of Alaska. Ten million gallons (40 million liters) of crude oil were spilled. The spill affected thousands of miles of coastline. Within days, thousands of animals had died, including up to 500,000 seabirds, more than 1,000 sea otters, 12 river otters, 300 harbor seals, and 22 killer whales. Twenty years later, thousands of gallons of oil remain in the sand, and the oil still affects the coastal ecosystem.

Cigarette Butts

Millions of cigarette butts are washed from city streets to the coast every day. Cigarette butts pollute the coast and kill wildlife. Birds and fish mistake butts for food and swallow them. The butts may block the animals' intestines. There are **toxins** in cigarette butts that poison animals, too.

Plastic Litter

Millions of tons of plastic litter is washed up on the world's coasts every year. Discarded plastic shopping bags are blown or washed to the coast from city streets. Some plastic waste comes from ships. Plastics take many years to break down and are a serious threat to coastal wildlife.

Plastic pollution affects biodiversity when animals eat the waste or become entangled in it. A leatherback turtle may mistake a plastic bag for a jellyfish and swallow it. The bag blocks the turtle's intestines, and it starves to death. Many animals become entangled in plastic waste, such as shopping bags, and are unable to hunt or to evade predators.

Did You Know?

Between 1999 and 2004, two hundred marine turtles were found entangled in fishing nets at Cape Arnhem, northern Australia. During two weeks in 2001, 600 fishing nets, 3,000 floats, 4,000 plastic bottles, and 3,000 sandals were collected from a nearby beach.

Marine turtles may become entangled in discarded plastic fishing nets.

BIODIVERSITY THREAT:
Climate Change

The world's average temperature is increasing in a process known as global warming. Global warming results in climate change, including severe storms and rising sea levels. This climate change is threatening coastal biodiversity.

Global Warming

Amounts of certain greenhouse gases, such as carbon dioxide, in Earth's atmosphere are increasing. Greenhouse gases trap heat in the atmosphere like glass traps heat in a greenhouse. An overall increase in temperature, called global warming, is causing changes to the climate. Some of these changes are affecting coasts.

Tropical Storms

Typhoons and hurricanes affect the coast. They whip up large waves, which flood coastal land, destroying habitats and crops, and causing soil to erode away. Scientists predict that global warming will not cause more frequent storms, but it will cause more intense storms. The effects on coastlines will be more extreme.

During a tropical storm, strong winds and heavy waves batter coastal areas.

Rising Sea Levels

As Earth's average temperature rises, the polar ice caps are shrinking. This causes sea levels to rise, threatening the future of many low-lying islands. Kiribati is a nation of low-lying islands in the Pacific. Many of its 95,000 people have had to relocate from the coast as the sea rises and intrudes on the land. Scientists predict that if sea levels continue to rise, Kiribati will be completely under water within one hundred years.

Rising sea levels threaten the biodiversity of many coasts around the world. Low-lying coastlines are at greatest risk. When seawater floods over land, it brings salt with it. Many plants cannot tolerate the salt and are killed. Salt-tolerant plants, such as samphire and saltbush, replace these plants. This change in habitat leads to a change in the species of animals that can live in these places.

Low-lying Funafuti Atoll, in Tuvalu, is slowly being covered by the sea.

Tuvalu

Tuvalu is a Pacific island nation with a population of 11,000. Its islands make up an area of just 10 square miles (26 sq km). In recent years, some very high tides, called king tides, have been the highest in history. Waves have flooded roads and made the soil too salty to grow crops.

Scientists predict that within fifty years all Tuvaluans will have to be evacuated and the islands will disappear altogether. The effect on biodiversity may not be so severe. Land-living animals will lose their habitat, but marine species will have more habitat.

Coastal Conservation

Conservation is the protection, preservation, and wise use of resources. Sometimes, the human use of coasts results in conservation problems. Research, regulations, and education are used to solve these problems and encourage coastal conservation.

Conservation Problems

Coasts are very important to the many species that live in and around them. They are also very important to people. The beach at Cape Hatteras, North Carolina, is used by turtles for nesting. It is also used by people for four-wheel driving. In situations such as this, the two uses pose a conservation problem.

The conservation of North Carolina coastal area is very important to the turtles' survival.

Research

Research surveys or studies are used to find out information about coasts, such as how coastal ecosystems work and how humans affect them. Research helps people work out ways to conserve coastal biodiversity.

At Cape Hatteras, loggerhead, flatback, and green turtles nest along the beach. On a typical summer weekend, about 2,000 vehicles are driven along the same beach by vacationers. Many people believe that this beach driving is harming the turtles. They argue that the turtles are disturbed by:

- collisions with cars
- the compacting of sand, which makes it too hard for hatchlings to dig themselves out of their nests
- streetlights, which confuse the hatchlings
- wheel tracks in the sand, which block the hatchlings' way to the sea.

The U.S. National Park Service manages the beach. They need to know how best to protect the turtles. To solve the problem, the National Park Service is conducting a scientific research study to find out how seriously beach driving affects turtles.

Some people believe that driving cars, trucks, and ATVs on the beach harms the turtles in the area.

Regulations

Once a research study is done, regulations or laws are passed. At Cape Hatteras, these regulations may be that beach driving is banned at night, between certain months, or along certain sections of beach. National Park Service officers would patrol the beach, and penalties would apply to people breaking these regulations.

Education

Good conservation plans involve education. When people understand how their actions affect biodiversity, they are more likely to cooperate and obey regulations. At Cape Hatteras, beach drivers and other people need to know how they can help protect the turtles.

CASE STUDY:
The Mediterranean Coast

Humans began settling the coast of the Mediterranean Sea about 3,000 years ago. Today, the human population is putting severe pressure on biodiversity.

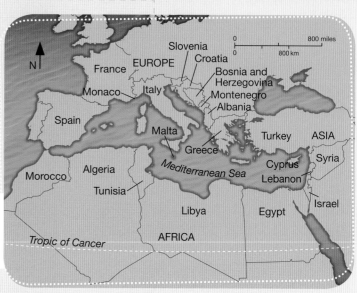

The Mediterranean coast is shared by countries in Africa, Asia, and Europe.

Tourism Pressures

About 110 million tourists visit the coast of the Mediterranean Sea every year, doubling the local population. The tourists are mainly Europeans who travel to the coast for summer holidays. In some areas, such as the Costa Brava in Spain, during the summer the population can increase to ten times its normal size.

Tourism along France's Mediterranean coast is worth $5 billion a year to the French economy. Spain earns even more from its coastal tourism. Because so much money can be made, **urban** development of the Mediterranean coast has continued at a fast pace. Wildlife habitats have been replaced with roads, buildings, and golf courses. Experts predict that the total number of tourists to the Mediterranean coast may double to 200 million a year by 2025.

Negative Effects of Tourism

In 1998, the World Wide Fund for Nature (WWF) conducted a research survey of Turkey's Mediterranean coast. The survey found that tourism had seriously affected 40 percent of the 1,526 miles (2,456 km) coastline. It found that half of the beach areas used by nesting marine turtles had been destroyed when sand was removed to make concrete for buildings and roads.

Threats to Mediterranean Biodiversity

The drainage of wetlands has occurred for hundreds of years along many parts of the Mediterranean coast. The European side of the Mediterranean coast has lost much of its undisturbed habitat and biodiversity has declined. Today, there are very few wetlands left and the threat to coastal biodiversity is greater than ever.

The wetlands of the Mediterranean are vitally important habitats for **migratory birds**. Scientists estimate that up to 2 billion migratory birds, from 150 species, live for part of the year in the Mediterranean wetlands or use the wetlands as rest areas on their migrations to and from Africa.

Loss of these wetlands would be catastrophic for migratory bird species, as well as for the fish and other species that live and breed in the wetlands.

Did You Know?

More than half of the 25,000 species of plants in the Mediterranean region are **endemic species**.

Dalmatian pelicans are migratory birds that nest and breed in Mediterranean wetlands.

Threats to the African Coast

On the African side of the Mediterranean Sea, the coast still has some undisturbed habitat where wildlife thrives. However, the threat from development remains. The Moulouya River estuary in Morocco is an important Mediterranean wetland. It is unaffected by tourism. There are plans to build a resort close to the estuary to attract tourists from Europe, so it may not be safe for much longer. Eighteen endangered species live in the estuary, including the Mediterranean monk seal and one of the rarest birds in Europe, the slender-billed curlew. An endangered flowering herb, *Spergularia embergeri*, is also found there.

The habitat of the critically endangered slender-billed curlew is threatened by plans to develop a vacation resort.

Protecting the Mediterranean Coast

Some conservation groups believe that governments are too slow to act to save important habitats along the Mediterranean coast. These groups are taking action of their own. The Italian WWF organization bought 77 square miles (200 sq km) of habitat along the coast of Tuscany, in Italy. In France, Conservatoire du littoral has bought 310 miles (500 km) of Mediterranean coast and wetlands.

Citizens and governments are also helping protect the coast. At the resort of Arene Cros, in southern France, residents' protests have stopped construction of hotels, apartments, and a new marina for 1,200 boats. The development threatened sea grass that is an important breeding habitat for fish.

Did You Know?

In France in 2008, an opinion poll found that 80 percent of people surveyed believed that greater government control of development in coastal areas was needed.

Many marinas have been built along the Mediterranean coast, destroying natural habitats.

What Is the Future of Coasts?

Human activities cause sudden, major changes to coasts. Most animals cannot cope with such rapid change. The future survival of coastal **species** depends on the creation of reserves where human activities are limited. The protection of coastal biodiversity requires action.

What Can You Do For Coasts?

You can help protect the coasts in several ways:

- Find out about coasts. Why are they important and what threatens them?

- Join a volunteer group that cleans up the beach or replants coastal areas.

- Become a responsible consumer. Buy products that have minimal packaging and do not litter.

- If you are concerned about coasts in your area, or in other areas, send a letter to or e-mail your local newspaper, your state congressperson, or local representative, and express your concerns. Know what you want to say, set out your arguments, be sure of your facts, and ask for a reply.

Useful Websites

🖥 **www.panda.org/what_we_do/where_we_work/mediterranean/about/marine/**
This website gives information about how the WWF is helping protect marine and coastal diversity in the Mediterranean.

🖥 **www.biodiversityhotspots.org**
This website has information about the richest and most threatened areas of biodiversity on Earth.

🖥 **www.iucnredlist.org**
The International Union for Conservation of Nature (IUCN) Red List has information about threatened plant and animal species.

Glossary

adapt   Change in order to survive.

algae   Simple marine plants without leaves.

ballast   Seawater that is taken on board a ship to keep it weighted and stable at sea when it is not carrying cargo.

carbon dioxide   A colorless and odorless gas produced by plants, animals, and the burning of coal and oil.

climate   The weather conditions in a certain region over a long period of time.

degradation   Erosion and breakdown of the land.

ecosystem   The living and nonliving things in a certain area and the interactions between them.

endemic species   Species found only in a particular area.

erosion   Wearing away of soil and rock by wind or water.

extinct   Having no living members.

genes   Segments of deoxyribonucleic acid (DNA) in the cells of a living thing, which determine characteristics.

habitats   Places where animals, plants, or other living things live.

heritage   Things we inherit and pass on to future generations.

interactions   Actions that are taken together or that affect each other.

invasive species   Nonnative species that negatively affect their new habitats.

kelp   Type of large brown seaweed.

marine   Of the sea.

migratory birds   Birds that fly from one part of the world to another, and back, each year.

mudflats   Areas of muddy shore that are left uncovered at low tide.

nutrients   Substances that are used by living things for growth.

organisms   Animals, plants, and other living things.

outcrops   Rock formations that are visible above the ground.

plankton   Microscopic organisms that drift in the sea.

predators   Animals that kill and eat other animals.

sewage   Human and animal waste.

silt   Fine sand, soil, and other materials carried by water and deposited as sediment.

species   A group of animals, plants, or other living things that share the same characteristics and can breed with one another.

toxins   Poisons.

urban   Of towns and cities.

urbanization   The development of towns and cities.

vegetation   Plants.

Index